KAMOSÉ presents

We Are
Kings and Queens

By Kareem Alexis

ISBN - 9780692776216

This book is dedicated to my children; Empress Krystal,
Empress Kasayah, and Emperor Kaleb. "We Are Kings
and Queens" is also dedicated to all the children and
young adults in the world that never received the
teachings that my children have received from me.
Now, these same stories are available for everyone.
Now, we can all look in the mirror, see royalty,
and feel empowered. In memory of the
goddess Dr. Frances Cress Welsing.

TABLE OF CONTENTS

Queen Nefertari (Ne-fer-tari) Merytmut was an Egyptian queen and the first of the Great Royal Wives of Ramesses the Great. Nefertari, meaning "beautiful companion", and Merytmut, meaning "beloved of (the goddess) Mut", is one of the best known queens next to Cleopatra, Nefertiti, and Hatsheput. Nefertari was highly educated and able to both read and write hieroglyphs, a very rare skill at the time. She used these skills in her diplomatic work, negotiating with other prominent royalties of the time.

Nefertari was the Nubian queen from 1292 to 1225 B.C. One of a many great Nubian queens, Nefertari is recognized as the queen who wed for peace. Her marriage to Ramesses II began strictly as a political move, a sharing of power between two leaders. But not only did it grow into one of the greatest royal love affairs in history, it brought the hundred year war between Nubia and Egypt to an end. Even today, a monument stands in Queen Nefertari's honor. In fact, the temple which Ramesses built for her at Abu Simbel is one of the largest and most beautiful structures ever built to honor a wife.

King Kamose (Kah-Mos), the 15th King of the 17th Dynasty, was the son of King Seqenenre Taa I and Queen Ahhotep. He ruled in the southernmost third of Egypt (Kemet). Kamose assumed the throne after the death of his father. Kamose's father, King Seqenenre Taa I, had been at war with the Hyksos (a group of Semitic settlers who had seized the northern part of Egypt in the 17th century BCE). Honoring the legacy of his father, Kamose continued the war to push out the invaders.

With his fleet and desert tribal troops from Nubia, he made a surprise attack against the southernmost Hyksos stronghold. Continuing his northward march, Kamose showed no mercy to the Egyptians who had made accommodations with the enemy. He also captured Hyksos ships laden with weapons and sailed past the Hyksos capital itself, in the eastern Nile River delta. On the way to attack the Hyksos, Kamose captured a messenger for the Hyksos who was carrying a message for the Kushite prince, urging him to attack Egypt from the rear. Kamose used the message to strategically plan an attack on the Hyksos and defeat the rebels. His name appears in Nubia, at the Second Nile Cataract, next to his brother, Ahmose, who succeeded him. In honor of King KAMOSE, there is a product line founded and created by Kareem Alexis called "Kamosé". The products are tea, lotion, soap, and lip balm made from all natural, organic, and non-GMO herbs, oils, and butters.

Queen Amina's family's wealth was derived from the trade of leather goods, cloth, salt, and horses. Amina chose to spend her time honing her military skills with the warriors of the Zazzau cavalry. This led to her eventually emerging as a leader of the Zazzau cavalry, during which time she accumulated great wealth and numerous military accolades from her battles.

The objective of Queen Amina initiating so many battles was to ensure safe passage for her soldiers, who handled and travelled with all her goods to be traded with other nations. This is how she boosted her kingdom's wealth and power.

Queen Amina fortified each of her military camps with an earthen wall. Then she would build towns and villages inside these walls for her soldiers and their families. The walls became known as Amina's Walls and many of them still remain in existence to this day.

Queen Amina expanded the territory of the Hausa people of North Africa to its largest borders in history. The expansion of Queen Amina's kingdom made it the trading centre for all of southern Hausaland. Spanning the traditional east-to-west trans-Saharan axis and guaranteeing the land named after her sister, Zaria's prosperity. Nigeria has immortalized Amina by erecting a statue of her riding a horse with a spear in her hand, in the centre of Lagos.

King Hannibal, the son of Hamilclar, was born in 247 B.C., in Carthage, North Africa. At a very young age, about 8 or 9, Hannibal accompanied his father in a battle against the Romans. Seventeen years later in 221 B.C., he became supreme commander of the peninsula. Hannibal had 80,000 infantry, 12,000 cavalry, and 40 African war elephants. He conquered major portions of Spain and France, and all of Italy.

In one battle, the Romans put 80,000 men on the field led by Scipio to defeat Hannibal. When Scipio attacked with his entire army, Hannibal had so studied the grounds that he arranged his African swordsmen and several large elephants to trample and slaughter them. King Hannibal is said to be the most strategic and greatest military leader in Africa of all time. He also had his own money with his face on one side and the image of an elephant on the other.

Queen Ana Nzingha (N-Zing-ga) Mbande was born in West Africa in 1583. A monarch of the Mbunde people, Queen Nzingha was a wise diplomat and excelled as a military leader, fighting against the Portuguese who were trying to expand the slave trade in Central Africa.

When the slave-hunting Portuguese attacked the army of her brother's kingdom, Nzingha was sent to negotiate the peace. She did so with astonishing skill and political tact. Although Nzingha met with the Portuguese several times, it was during the first meeting that she was not offered a seat, so the men with her got on their hands and knees and she sat on their backs. Nzingha assumed the throne in 1626 after the death of her brother, King Ngolo Mbande.

Forming her own army, Nzingha waged war against the Portuguese for nearly 30 years. These battles were a unique moment in colonial history as Nzingha allied her nation with the Dutch, marking the first African-European alliance against a European oppressor.

Nzingha continued to have considerable influence among her subjects because of her quest for freedom and relentless drive to bring peace to her people. Nzingha remains a great symbol of inspiration to stand up to our oppressors.

King Mansa Musa of Mali was an important Malian King, ruling from 1312 to 1337. He was a master businessman and economist. He obtained his wealth through Mali's supply of gold, salt, and ivory. He was estimated to have been worth the equivalent of $400 billion in today's currency, making him the richest man in the world.

Musa was also a major influence on the University of Timbuktu, the world's first university and major learning institution for not just Africa, but the world. Timbuktu became a meeting place of poets, scholars, and artists of Africa and the Middle East. Even after Mali's decline, Timbuktu remained the major learning center of Africa for many years.

Musa remains most famous for his pilgrimage to Mecca in 1324. During his pilgrimage, he stopped in the City of Cairo, Egypt (Kemet) and gave gifts of gold. Musa's generosity resulted in an economic upset causing the price of metal to decrease. This was the only event in history where a man so rich could cause such an economic upset to another country.

The Queen of Sheba, also referred to in some text as Makeda (Ma-key-da), is honored for her journey to Jerusalem. The Queen of Sheba is said to have taken a long and difficult journey to Jerusalem to learn from the wisdom of the great King Solomon. Makeda and King Solomon were equally impressed with each other. Out of this relationship was born a son, Menelik I.

It is said that the king of kings, the conquering lion of Judah, Haile Selassie I, the former Emperor of Ethiopia, comes from this lineage. This queen is said to have reigned over Sheba and Arabia, as well as, Ethiopia. The Queen of Sheba's capital was Debra Makeda, which she built for herself.

In Ethiopia's church of Aksum, there is a copy of what is said to be one of the Tables of Law that Solomon gave to Menelik I. The story of the Queen of Sheba is deeply cherished in Ethiopia as part of the national heritage. This African queen is mentioned in two holy books, the Bible and the Quran.

King Shaka of the Zulus, the son of Zulu Chief Senzangakhona and his wife Nandi, was born in 1787. After the death of his father, Shaka commenced to rule around 1818. A strong leader and military innovator, Shaka is noted for revolutionizing 19th century Bantu warfare. Shaka invented the "assegai", a short stabbing spear that would be used by his men in close contact battle.

Shaka organized and trained his men to use standardized weapons and special tactics. He marched his soldiers in tight formation, by using spears and large shields to fend off the enemies. Shaka and his fierce Zulu warriors were able to defeat many European invasions by only using their spears and shields. The Europeans were armed with hand guns and rifles. Over the years, Shaka's troops earned such a reputation that many enemies would flee at the site of them.

Shaka built a small Zulu tribe into a powerful nation of more than a million people and united all tribes in South Africa against European colonial rule. The Zulu nation continued to use Shaka's innovations in wars after his death.

In honor of his bravery and courage, there are many hotels, restaurants, a theme park, and a movie named after him.

Queen Yaa Asantewaa (Yah-AH-San-Te-Wah) is known as the greatest and fiercest female leader in West Africa. She was a mother, farmer, human rights activist, Queen, and a leader. Yaa Asantewaa was appointed the Queen Mother of Ejisua in the Ashanti Empire by her brother, Nana Akwasi Afrane Okpese, the ruler of Ejisua.

In 1900, Yaa Asantewaa led an army to protect the Golden Stool – the supreme symbol of the sovereignty and independence of the Ashanti kingdom. This is known as the "War of the Golden Stool" against the British. Yaa Asantewaa led and fought very bravely and won many victories. The "War of the Golden Stool" was the last war in West Africa (modern day Ghana) to be led by a woman.

Queen Mother Yaa Asantewaa was born in 1840. She is honored in West Africa as the greatest and most courageous African woman to date. Yaa Asantewaa's legacy lives on with a school named in her honor, Yaa Asantewaa Girls' Secondary School.

King Haile Selassie I rose to become emperor of Ethiopia and was proclaimed "King of Kings". Outside of Ethiopia, he received tremendous honor and respect. He was the longest-serving head of state in power and he was often given precedence over all other leaders at state events.

Halie Selassie is worshipped as God incarnate among followers of the Rastafari movement. He is viewed as the messiah who will lead the peoples of Africa and the African diaspora to freedom. His title is the "Conquering Lion of the Tribe of Judah". His name, Haile Selassie, means "Power of the Trinity".

Haile Selassie I visited Jamaica on April 21, 1966. Hearing that the King who they considered to be a messiah was coming to the island, hundreds of thousands of Rastafarians from all over Jamaica went to see him at Palisadoes Airport in Kingston.

Haile Selassie I claimed direct descent from Makeda, known as the Queen of Sheba, and King Solomon. All monarchs must trace their lineage to Menelik I, who was the offspring of King Solomon and the Queen of Sheba.

You Are Royalty

Kareem Alexis is the owner of Kamose LLC
(www.kamose.me (http://www.kamose.me)), which
provides all natural, organic, and holistic products
to the world. He created "We Are Kings and Queens"
as another way to free our minds of lies and toxic
content. Also to empower the youth who do not
always get to see positive images of themselves in
our society. Just like the products at www.kamose.
me (http://www.kamose.me), "We Are Kings and
Queens" was created to provide true organic,
holistic, and uplifting nourishment for the mind.

Dedicated to the memory of the Great Goddess
Dr. Francess Cress Welsing.

We are King and Queens volume 2 coming soon.

Contact:
Email: kamoseshea@gmail.com
(mailto:kamoseshea@gmail.com)
Facebook: Kamose LLC
Twitter: Kamose LLC
Website: www.kamose.me (http://www.kamose.me)

CPSIA information can be obtained
at www.ICGtesting.com
Printed in the USA
LVRC02n1424110817
544661LV00015B/62